THE WORLD OF WHALES

by Dina Anastasio

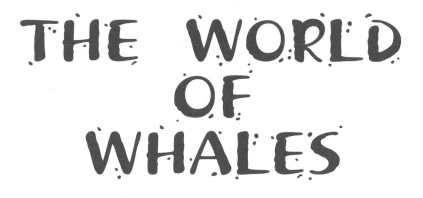

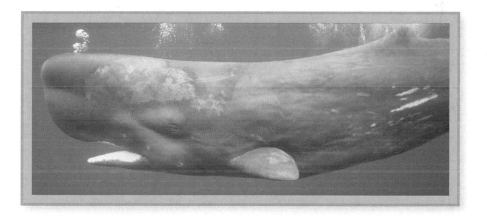

Table of Contents

Introduction

Where do some of the largest mammals in the world live? They live under water. Whales spend their whole lives in the ocean.

Whales never stop swimming. Most of the time, they swim in groups. Sometimes whales play. Then they jump out of the water and dive back in. They slap their fins against the water and do belly flops. Whales even sing underwater.

How many different kinds of whales are there? What kinds of food do they eat? You will find the answers to these questions in this book.

Whales can jump far out of the water. After ↻ this picture was taken, this whale dove back under the water.

⌂ Baby whales, called calves, stay close to their mothers until they can take care of themselves.

Chapter 1
The Life of Whales

Whales live in groups called pods. The pod lives, eats, and travels together. In most pods, the whales are all part of the same family. But some pods are made of friends. A group of whale mothers and their calves can be a pod. Once in a while, whales move to different pods. But this does not happen very often.

⊙ This lucky explorer came across a pod of orcas.

All whales live in the sea. Some whales stay in one place. For other whales, home is wherever they are at that time.

Whales never stop moving, even when they are sleeping. How do they do this? Many scientists believe that whales take a short nap. Then they wake up and breathe. And then they take another nap. Some whales even sleep with one eye open. They watch for **predators** with their open eye.

Blowholes

A whale breathes through a **blowhole** in its skull. What comes out may look like water, but it's really more like mist. This mist is called "blow."

Whales spend half the year eating. During the rest of the year, these massive animals eat very little. Whales eat mostly during the summer months. Some whales feed on the ocean floor. Others feed near the surface.

Whales have a unique way to save food for later. They change food into a <u>layer</u> of fat, called blubber, under their skin. Blubber keeps whales warm when they are in cold water and gives them energy.

<u>layer</u>: a line, or fold

How Tall Are They?

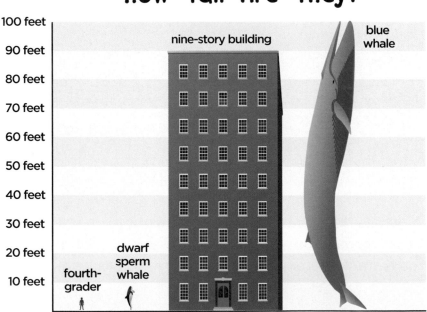

↻ The smallest whale is the dwarf sperm whale. The biggest whale is the blue whale. The blue whale is the largest animal on Earth.

Toothed vs. Baleen

There are two important groups of whales. Toothed whales have teeth. They catch fish with their teeth. **Baleen** whales don't have teeth. They scoop up tangles of food and seawater in their mouths. The baleen, which is like a comb, separates the food from the seawater.

⊕ The sperm whale is the largest toothed whale.

⊕ Humpback whales are baleen whales.

⌂ The beluga whale is known as the "sea canary." It can make many different sounds.

Did you know that whales <u>can</u> talk to each other? They make different sounds for different reasons. They use sounds to find mates. Mother whales use certain sounds to find their calves.

Toothed whales click and whistle to locate food. Baleen whales make moaning, snoring, and rumbling noises. Humpback whales sing in the warm waters where they spend the breeding season. We don't know why whales sing. Maybe they sing love songs. Maybe they are telling other whales to go away.

Clue: <u>Can</u> is a homograph. It has more than one meaning. Can you think of different meanings of this word? You can use a dictionary for help.

Echolocation

Toothed whales use **echolocation** to find food. When whales echolocate, they make a clicking sound. The clicking sounds bounces off the object. The whales listen to how much time it takes the echo to travel back to them. If it takes a long time, dinner is far away. If it takes only a second or so, the prey is nearby.

Before humpback whales sing, they swim up to the surface and take a few breaths. Then they dive under the water and start to sing. They do not move when they sing. Their underwater songs can be heard from miles away. Sometimes they sing for 30 minutes without stopping.

↻ The song of the right whale can be heard for miles.

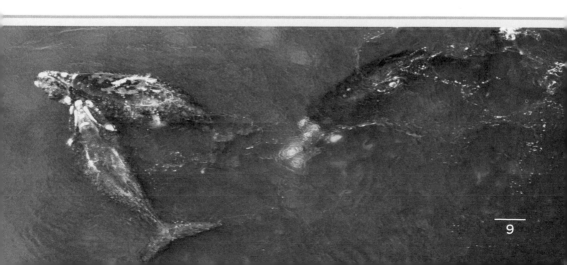

Chapter 2
Whale Families

Whale pods may be friends or families. The stongest bond, or tie, is between a mother and <u>her</u> calf. Some mothers and their calves stay together forever. The orca is one **species** where the mother and calf never separate.

Clue: <u>Her</u> is a possessive pronoun. Can you find another possessive pronoun on this page?

☺ Many pods include grandmothers, mothers, and calves.

In some species, older male calves do leave their mothers. The female calves stay. Male sperm whales stay until they are about five years old. After that, they take care of themselves. They go to places where it is easy to find food. They look for a new pod. Usually the young males join other young males and stay in that pod for the next 40 years. When sperm whales grow old, they usually leave the pod and live alone in deeper waters.

Whale Social Groups

Social groups, from smallest to largest:

A *maternal pod* is a mother whale and her calf.

A *pod* is a group of whales that lives together.

A *clan* is a group of pods that sometimes travels together.

A *community* is a group of clans.

Whales that stay in groups take care of each other. They help other members of their pod as they travel long distances. Like other animals, they play, fight, and show love to each other. Sometimes they form small groups in their pods called sub-pods.

Most whales are shy and gentle. When a sperm whale wants to get closer to one of the whales in her pod, she rubs up against it. When whales of the same species want to show they care, they stroke, or pat, each other with their fins. Mothers and calves stroke each other too.

Beluga Whales

About 10 beluga whales live together in a pod. Like other species of whales, several pods travel together when they move from place to place.

↻ Whales may stroke each other to show feelings.

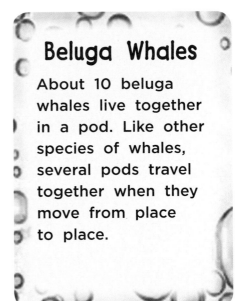

Chapter 3
Moving and Playing

Have you ever seen whales playing? They jump, <u>thrash</u>, and throw themselves out of the water. They slap their fins and **flukes** and do belly flops. What do all these twirls, slaps, and jumps mean? Whale watchers often wonder if whales are looking for food, playing, or searching for a mate. It's hard to know unless you are a whale.

<u>thrash</u>: to move wildly

↻ Orcas are great gymnasts.

Different whales like different games. Pilot whales play "follow the leader." They live in very large pods. Often they form lines that lead fishermen toward <u>schools</u> of fish. However, sometimes pilot whales follow their leader onto a beach. No one knows why this happens. Perhaps something goes wrong with the leader's echolocation. Maybe the leader swims too close to shore and cannot turn back. Whatever the reason, pilot whales will follow their leader anywhere.

<u>schools</u>: large numbers of fish swimming together

↻ The dorsal, or back, fins of these pilot whales are above the water.

Whale Games

⟳ Breaching: Whales jump out of the water, spin, and crash backward or sideways when they come back down.

Fluking: Whales ⟳ raise their tails before they dive down into the water. Fluking is often done by large whales, like the massive blues.

⟳ Sailing: Whales move with their heads down and their tails fluking above the surface.

⟲ Body Rolling: Whales roll onto their backs and swim.

Whales are always moving. Some travel a very long way. Others just swim around in a small area. Whales even "carry" their young. A calf is carried along in the water <u>current</u> created by its mother as she swims. That's how calves keep up with the rest of the pod.

Some whales **migrate** from one area to another. Blue whales migrate thousands of miles every year. They spend winter in warm waters where their young are born. In the summer, they migrate to cooler waters, where it's easier to find food.

<u>current</u>: water or air moving in one direction

☪ It helps to be carried along in a water current.

California gray whales migrate even farther. Every year they swim about 10,000 miles (16,093 km) round trip between Mexico and the Bering Sea, near Alaska.

round trip: a trip from one place to another place and then back

Spy-Hopping

Sometimes a whale needs to know where it is or what the weather is. It pops its head up above the surface. This is called spy-hopping.

Conclusion

In the ocean, pods of whales are swimming. They are searching for food, caring for their calves, and playing whale games.

Many people want politicians to make laws that protect whales. It is easy to understand why people would want to help these caring, intelligent, and amazing animals. Somewhere gray whales are swimming thousands of miles in order to find food. Orcas are slapping their flukes. Pilot whales are playing "follow the leader." If you listen closely, you might even hear a humpback whale singing a song.

⊙ Whales live, play, and sing all over the world.

Glossary

baleen one of two large groups of whales. Baleen whales have two blowholes and a comb-like plate in their mouths that helps them gather food from seawater. *(page 7)*

blowhole a hole on the top of the head of whales, dolphins, and porpoises *(page 5)*

echolocation a way to find the location of something by measuring how long it takes an echo to return from it *(page 9)*

flukes the two flat tail pieces of a whale, dolphin, or porpoise *(page 13)*

migrate to move from one place to another *(page 16)*

predators animals that live by hunting other animals for food *(page 5)*

species a group of animals or plants that are alike in many ways *(page 10)*

Index

Comprehension Check

Summarize

Complete a Sequence Chart with the class. Summarize the story. You can use the chart to help you organize your ideas.

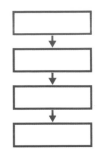

Think and Compare

1. Look at pages 10–11. Where does a male sperm whale live when it is a calf? Where does it live when it is old? *(Identify Sequence of Events)*

2. Whales play in all kinds of ways. How do whales play like you do? How do they play differently? *(Analyze)*

3. Do you think it is important to protect whales? Why or why not? Would you like to go whale watching someday? *(Evaluate)*